Dedication

To the OG Pen-to-Paper kids.

This Book Belongs To

____

Introduction

Like all of us, after the COVID-19 Pandemic, I was in need of healing. Also, like many of you, what happened for me after the pandemic was not a months long, tranquil retreat accompanied by hours of well-researched and meaningful therapy. Unfortunately, again, like the collective, I went through more hardships and more trials of trust and turmoil.

Basically it comes down to this: WE ALL NEED HEALING. And like LOADS of it. Like heaping, grandma's homecooking at the holidays sized portions of healing are needed, folks. Because there's not just one collective hardship, there are many and it is continuous. And the prospect of that is super scary and makes me want to retreat into a cave of Ben and Jerry's ice cream and endless movies. While that sounds nice, it's not what complete healing looks like. Not that I have that figured out, but I for sure have figured out that it's not ice cream/movie eternal hermit cave. Disappointing, I know.

I knew I needed healing, but I wasn't sure of the timing on when to begin. I think I was waiting on the obstacles to stop and then I would go and solve all my problems in one go. You know, like when you bring your car into the shop and finally fork over a mini-life savings so you can get all the repairs and care you're supposed to do as a responsible person. How pragmatic of me, I know. But obviously, that doesn't work. Much like the beat in the kid's movie *Trolls*, the pain and hardships don't stop. OH LORDY! Don't stop reading here! The good news is, you can create a lot of your own healing momentum by getting out of yourself, connecting with others, nature, and your surroundings, and diving into your own creative pursuits.

This isn't an end-all- be-all creative fix and it's not an overnight solution. It's a boost. A kick in the pants. A slingshot start. An encouraging pep talk from a best friend at brunch. It's a short order manual for getting the whimsy and blood moving and the pen dancing.

How to Read this Book

You've already proved to be a savvy imp by even picking up a book on poetry and creative momentum so trust your own instincts but here's how the book was designed:

The book alternates between poems and "side quests & shenanigans". "Side quests & shenanigans" are designed to break up the reading of poetry and help jumpstart your own writing and creativity. They aren't all writing-centered, but can be used as fuel for writing. In every case, it's an opportunity to get out of your head, try new creative approaches, and regain the zest and appreciation for the life and community around us. Because let's be honest, the life and community around us can sometimes be trying. Or can feel isolating. Perhaps there's not a visible community for yourself yet. My hope is, like me, once you get out there, you'll either see you're not alone or a path for creating community is just shy one element from bursting into life: you!

Just so we're all on the same page, "shenanigans" are mild mischief one and their comrades might get up to. The hope with a shenanigan is that it leads to a burst of excitement or joy and those sharing in the shenanigan are further bonded.

A "side quest" is a short errand or practice that is separate from the "main plot" of your life. But like a good side story, a "side quest" usually brings a break from the mundane, a necessary experience, or a reprieve from the main complexity at hand. A good side quest can provide a short refuge, but it can also provide greater perspective for the experience.

When folks spout off cliches like "it's the small things"- I think of "side quests and shenanigans". These are the experiences that may not be in my family photo album, but they steadily build friendships and wisdom. They offer an exciting garnish to the day, the spice and zest of life. Side quests and shenanigans are the small moments that add up to big connections and a larger perspective, if we allow it.

Josh

A NOTE FROM JES

Ways to use this book

There are many ways to use this book, but the main thing is to *use* it. Write in it, dog ear the pages, scribble doodles.

We hope you take it with you on all your *side quests* and make notes about your *shenanigans*.

Most importantly, be brave. It takes courage to create. To put pen to paper and make a specific mark. A mark that only you have ever made. With the myriad of things we cannot control, this is one thing we can. Be courageous in the quests and in your craft.

We have creativity and we have each other. Through this book we can all grow and become bold in our curiosity. Tenacious in our craft. Lighthearted a few moments a day.

You are worth the time it takes to find laughter and silliness.

-Jes

Content Warnings: No content or trigger warnings have been noted by the authors, but please protect your mental health and if any of the prompts make you uncomfortable, skip them and keep your peace.

Table of Contents

Unsolicited Advice to New Poets

You will need calluses on the side
of your heart where you take rejection

You need to be
deranged flamingo, prancing confident.
Come with peacock screeching ego

You don't have to be without
fear, anxiety, or doubt
Your hunger just has to be more.

Poetry will not be taking the high road
It will take tunnels and portals
It will simply appear

Poetry will break shackles
Poetry will break sin
Poetry will birth you
Poetry will lift you up to the sun

Poetry comes in avalanches,
self-created monumental messes.

Poetry comes in pebbles
one truthful, sturdy stone at a time.

You better listen to the muse
Listen to instigators
Listen to ancestors
Listen to the river
You better listen to the
Muse

Be ten toes
for your craft, your community
Arm yourself
with pens, paper,
folders - digital &
otherwise.

Commune with the moon
Pull flowers from your mouth

If the bastards are still waking up
Send truth on the speaker
Like deeper medicine
You tired? Lean on the mic
Like Billie Holiday
Just let the song play

Your fuel is love
Your fuel is spite
Your fuel is truth
And your fuel is
your fuel & it's right
You better listen to the Muse

Cling to friends, caffeine,
and bread.
Take 2 vinyl and
A walk around the creek
And call me in the morning

You better listen to the Muse
And the Muse said MOVE

Invent a word.

Poetry can fit into a rigid structure with syllabic rules, rhyming rules, meter rules. But it can also be silly. Think of the sing-songy rhymes you got to play with when you were a kid. I like to oat oat oat opples and bonobos. (IYKYK). Get out of the box our grammar rules have set for us and play with sounds and definitions.

> Tip: Use a Scrabble or Boggle set and toss letters around until something sounds like a word. Start there and make up the definition after.

Status Update

My current political stance is:
How will this help a mother?

Lately, I have strummed strings
into song, wrestled words
into story.

My current dance move of choice is:
float.

My toxic trait is keeping tallies of my
efforts until an arbitrary counter sounds an
alarm in my head, telling me I've earned some rest.

My favorite snack is my wife.
My favorite pastime is flirting with
microphones.

I want to master the art of the lazy afternoon,
set myself to slow. Know the tempo of
waving grass in the sun.

Go on a drive and sing-along to your favorite songs.

Make a mix-tape for yourself. Sure, the music might be delivered through an app, but write it out. Make a playlist on a scrap piece of notebook paper, give it a title, doodle around the edges. Go for a drive. Music helps connect us with parts of ourselves that words alone can't reach. Roll down the windows. Drive until the playlist loops back around to the start. Do you want to keep driving? How does it feel to go for the sake of just going?

In Times of Fools

Dear Lord,
Make it make sense
When such catastrophic
Foolishness sees such
Golden days. When
Fools unabashed
In their venom, bold in
Their villany. Make it

Make sense. Or make the
Whip to clear the temple
Visible and vigilant.
Forgive these perilous moments
When my doubts and arrows
Are coaxed quicker
than the magic of my love

Throw rocks in the creek/river/pond/lake.

There is something inherently comforting about creating ripples that expand across the water. Where do they stop and start? What happens when you throw two rocks away from each other and the ripples meet? Find the perfect rock. The smoothest. The roughest. The one that looks like a lil' guy. Does it spark something in you to throw hard with no destructive intentions?

> Tip: Wear clothes that can get soggy or muddy. Dip a toe in if you're feeling adventurous.

Morning Poem

It's another morning waking up
Feeling like a bog-inhabiting
cryptid. If you're going to be
a monster, it helps
to be a powerful one.

I'm asking my morning coffee to cure
all the problems: physical and existential.
a tall order for what is essentially
hot bean juice.

It helps to think of it as a magic potion.

I am new and improved.
I have a coffee mug that says so.

I have ideas in my hair,
words spilling in my lattes.

Shattered. Laced in gold.
It helps to be kintsugi confident.

Go play air hockey.

Your plan may go something like this: Step one: find a place to play air hockey. Step two: find a friend. Step three: challenge them to a game of air hockey with high stakes. The winner buys ice cream or smoothies or slushies. Air hockey doesn't exist in a vacuum, so where are you? Is it fun? Frustrating? Nostalgic? Will you go for three rounds or stop at one?

Tulip

when my veins are coffee.
slot machine eyes, tongue
of downhill spokes.
days when my speed
seems set to palpate.

on these days, Lord
remind me
how long the tree takes
to see over the hill

remind me to bloom
like the tulip, sown
In the dark, no promise
Of the sunshine, only
To catapult color at
Spring's hello

as if to say, "this joy
was here all along." love was
just busy growing.

Give someone flowers.

Where are you going to get the flowers? Are you going to pick your own? Go buy some at the local florist? Who are you giving them to? Someone shared (we tried to find the source but no luck, so this is purely anecdotal), that a large number of men never get flowers until their funeral. Consider spreading flowery love to someone who might not get flowers often or ever. Who else is missing out?

I Want You to Have a Relationship with Hope

Just because you're an adult,
doesn't mean you're any less deserving
of recess, a nap, and a weekly trip to the library.

You are a fajita skillet of a person,
don't quiet your sizzle for anyone.

Think about all the mushy bananas
turned themselves into delicious bread.
You can do that with your life.

Cover a giant space in sidewalk chalk.

Maybe do this in a park and bring a bucket of chalk so passersby can join in. Does it evoke memories? Did you play with chalk as a child? How does it feel, making your mark on a space, but knowing it will wash away during the next rainfall? Were you too ambitious in the space you chose? Was it too small?

Self-Care Plan

Step 1: Rest
Become the Sleepy-Time-Tea bear. Hibernate so that when you emerge the townspeople think you are a mythical creature, freshly emerged to commit terrible prophecy.

Step 2: Do Less
Take stillness long enough to feel the sun kiss your forehead and silence long enough to hear that tiny voice in your head remind you:
"Hey, you're an adorable badass. Keep going."

Step 3: Have Faith
Not all of life can be fried chicken & loop-de-loop roller coasters.
But if you run at life with pantsless, Winnie-the-Pooh-like enthusiasm you might get something sweeter than honey.

Step 4: Bask in the Small Glories
Three cheers that someone convinced
normal people to let donuts be a breakfast food.

Buy a physical piece of music from a local record/music store.

So much of our music intake is digital. We can tap on a music app and let the algorithm take over. Don't let it. Buy something physical. Something you hold and intentionally play. An album you choose to consume in the way the artists intended. Not as a clip on a social media short, but as a whole piece of art and creation.

> **Tip:** Need a tapedeck or cd player? Pawnshops are a great place to pick up used ones!

In a Parking Lot in Tulsa

This city's skyline has cathedrals for teeth and bridges for curves.
Girl was born to dance and isn't allowed to.

I take a knife to my poems. Trim them up like a barber until the lines are clean.

Scraps of my consonants & vowels in the floorboard.

Fresh pages made Sunday presentable.

The poet is an animal who wishes to perform open heart surgery with words while simultaneously operating on themselves.

Continually asking: do these words make my heart look pretty?

Write an ode to something you love.

There are infinite ways to love. Is it the love of your pet? Your children? The really great rock you found when you were throwing rocks in the creek that you decided to keep in your pocket? A meal? A partner? Friend group. This ode can be to anything that you cherish or adore or crave.

> **Tip:** If you can't nail down one subject, make it a list poem and reflect on step four of the poem *Self-Care Plan*.

You're Home

Baby, change the song
And come
Sit closer to me

Here, give me your phone
Let me change everyone
In your contacts to "Atari" and "Nintendo"
Because they play too much

The day has
Given you blues
But i give you bread

Put your troubles in my hand
I tuck you in with inside jokes
Careful lips

Head, meet pillow
Heart, meet rest
You are home

Make a fire.

First, be safe about this. As I write it, there is a wind advisory and any fires outdoors are going to burn whole fields to the ground if we're not careful. "Make a fire" doesn't have to mean outdoors in a firepit or in the hearth of your grandma's home. It can be a single candle, lit with intention. Kindling can be small sticks or crumpled pages of a letter that no longer serves you. Fire is fleeting and yet makes a mark everywhere it goes. Do you have memories of fires? Positive or negative? Did you know that potassium burns purple?

Cast Iron

I have two cast iron skillets
I've been seasoning with
weekly meals and tenderness
for what will equal 4 childhoods.

I will pass down a history
of culinary comedy and love songs
chopped, diced, sautéed, and roasted.

My children will hear the hymns
of my kitchen each time they
sear a steak. A legacy of dancing
sock-footed, stove front, fighting
off some kind of hunger.

Learn a recipe from a family member.

Is it one that you've tasted a hundred times at every gathering or celebration or holiday, but you don't know quite what it is that makes it taste the way it does? Recipes and tastes hold powers through generations. Is it something your aunt learned from her father who learned from his cousin who learned it from ancestors further back. What does it feel like to eat the food you've made? To share a meal with a loved one?

My Champion is a Grandma Named Betty

She's 4 foot nothing
Doesn't let you leave the breakfast table
Unless you are too many biscuits deep

Full in belly, yes, but fed in the heart
No one is in your corner like grandma
My blood elders have passed on to Glory
But my wife's Gigi has picked up the story

She claims me, what's more
Knows my name
Tells me I'm good
Tells me to straighten up, eat more
Do better
Keep at it
Doesn't let me leave
The table until I am
Full in biscuit, yes, but
Full in spirit more

Call someone who looked out for you and thank them.

There is no statute of limitations on gratitude. I once found a stack of wedding thank you notes I'd written and never mailed when cleaning out a bedroom five years later. I still sent them (mostly for the bit, but regardless). It's easy to forget to show gratitude when someone looked out for you. Whether because of an oversight, or because the clarity of recognizing their help took time to see through the settling dust. Swallow your pride and give them a call.

Bring Back Jousting

Jousting offers so much.
First, the word itself. Say it-
thrust it forward, out of your mouth
like a sword.

Jousting offers men exploding
off of horses, struck and humbled.
Galloping punctuated with a crash.

Jousting offers the drama of armor.

Does anything in your life make you
want to climb a 900 pound animal
and charge, valiant-stupid forward?

To be so inspired might be the
lance point of it all.

Go eavesdrop/ear hustle a conversation in public for a story/poem prompt.

Like a bird watcher on the prairie, writers lurk in the corners of coffee shops and in grocery stores, peering across their mugs and carts, gathering information about the creatures conversing throughout the rooms. Will they overhear sweet missives between newly dating youths? Will a lawyer complain about a client? Will a mom be at her wit's end, begging a wriggly toddler to calm down long enough for her to finish her chai latte?

$500 and a Day Off

I want to give you $500 and a day off.
Spend it on frivolity- it's only a stanza
you're here so make it count. Make time

to play and rest, and be decadent. I want
to watch you spend $500 on not survival,
or bills, or hidden fees, or car repairs.

What does $500 worth of pizza rolls look like?
For $500: What kind of animal can we pet?
What kind of animal can we call our own?

How many school lunch accounts could we pay off?
Let's see what $500 worth of poetry books looks like
then give them away to strangers on the street.

Let's buy $500 worth of Nerf guns, snow cones, and
tacos and pretend it's always July. Let's deliver $500
worth of champagne to ER nurses. Let's go buy a

donut and tip $498.91. I hate that happiness here
is a war's worth of pain and pennies.

Donate stuffed animals from the second-hand store to a children's hospital or a shelter.

What was your favorite stuffed animal in your childhood? Do you still have it? What did it mean to you? Think about the impact a small gesture can have on someone hurting. Even if you just imagine it and don't see it.

Tip: Before taking donations, check the organization websites to find out what they have identified as a need. They may not need/accept stuffed animals, so follow their donation guidelines.

Nature Documentary

A good nature show takes you to places you can't afford to travel
A good nature show displays creatures you've never seen
A nature we can't leash or pet or groom
A nature we can't traverse
A good nature show makes you forget about 401(k)s and credit cards
A good nature show makes you root for the predator
A good nature show reminds you this can all go away
A good nature show puts your kids to sleep or at least makes them drowsy and available to dream
Of a nature where we stay outside for keeps

Spend an entire day looking for the most interesting bug and/or tree.

Snap pictures as you go to narrow down the most interesting one like a basketball tournament bracket. Ask for input from a friend or a stranger at the spot you're exploring. Which is more interesting, A or B? B or C? C or A? Back and forth until one comes out the clear champion bug or tree. Make it your phone background. Remind yourself of the process of discernment.

Ancestors

When
my grandmas
were laid low,

their
voices appeared
in my head

One
of them
wants me to

take
a blue
hymnal across the

backside
of any
preacher who makes

more
than their
average community member.

One
of them
wants me to

pick
up the
poem the way

she
picked up
a pen, her

mother
a paintbrush.
This poem does

Both
but I

like to listen

To
them gab
for hours in

The
old way
about good movies

With
leading men
sporting jackets &

Tailored
trousers, we
all swoon for

Cary
Grant &
the way he

Could
get into
Just enough trouble

To
make him
a better man

I'm
not ready
for extinction

I'm
too pretty
to be fossilized

I'm
too animated
to be butterfly

behind
glass

Read to a class/rest home.

Being read to is one of the loveliest experiences. To share a story with a group of people is a method of connecting that is hard to beat. We remember bedtimes when our grownups told us stories. Favorite teachers who would quiet the whole room and spend thirty minutes reading while you begged for just one more chapter. Volunteer to be the guest reader at your kid or niece or nephew or god kid's school and choose a favorite of yours to read so they can feel the energy. Visit a care home and offer to read to a resident, trusting that the workers will place you in the right room.

"LET'S GET MOVING"

my empathy muscle
can deadlift 500
pounds with a
Ronnie Coleman
"YEEAAAAH
BUUUUDDDYYYY"

yes, it's resulted
in many mornings
of sore muscles &
calluses

But my forgiveness
seems selective:
For the rich,
my heart seems
stuck to the couch.

I yell, encourage,
blast hits from the 80's,
give my best Richard Simmons-
implore shuffle with sweatbands
and shaking enthusiasm.

the heart simply scowls
back in salty retribution.

I let my heart believe it's in a movie.

My heart believes this is the montage
where it runs up the Philadelphia stairs.

My heart believes this is the part
where the Viking warrior goes from
grinding his axe to wielding it.

I remind my heart
Rocky loses and Valhalla
means we're dead.

My heart grumbles,
kicks a rock,
goes back to deadlifting.

I say, "3 more sets…until you let go."
What comes out after will be
worth the sweat & labor.

Find something in your home to trade for another item with a friend or simply give it away.

When I ran this prompt through ChatGPT and it said. JUST MAKING SURE YOU WERE STILL READING. Don't use AI, it's killing the planet, raising utility costs, lining the pockets of billionaires and turning our collective brains into a smooth, hollow rock. Okay, rant over.

This prompt makes me want to find the most haunted looking item in my house and gift it to a friend by just leaving it on their doorstep, ringing the bell and running away. But that's just one way to interpret it. Is there something that isn't serving you anymore, but could be used by someone else?

Animalist

I am newly devout
Confident in conviction
Faithful in following
My animal urges

Self care is shrieking.
Honor your howl.
Climb the cacophony of
the tops of your chaos.

Those wandering & wily
parts of you? Keep them.

Deliver us from dogma-
Oh Holy Creator Spirit
Prayers are in my
Climbing calluses

You have the doctrine
Of tears and panting
In throats and places
Of the soul. There
is the golden bucking
Of corporate yokes

I like you best with
raised antlers-rearing
in your beautiful wrath
A religion of resistance.
healthy hackles, a sign of
living wind to wind.

Climb a tree.

Or at least lay under one. Things feel different ten feet above the grass. (Or three, don't hurt yourself). There have been trees in your life to remember. To thank. To mourn. How does the time of year change how the tree affects you?

The Sun Drinkers

Sun drinkers
Sun pleasers
Swimming themselves happy

Finding poems
at the bottom of the pool
and the top of
doing nothing but listening

Sno cone eaters
Day trippers
Laughing languid
Through sun dangerous hours

mirth is a passion, is a craft,
mirth is ignorant, is always time
well spent. is a choice
when the summer is suffocating.

Moon swallowers
Record players
Making trouble
Making love
Making do

with nocturnal hours left
before fresh news cycles,
fresh kill. Fresh fruit
in your drink
to keep the blues away.

Tiny umbrellas
Tropical delight
only need a daydream
to get there

Escape was always a part of survival.

**Play hooky. We work too much. Life is too short.
Goof off.**

No really. Find a way to do this. It can be hard. But there are ways. Switch a shift with someone at a time of day you usually work. Call in for a mental health day in the middle of the week. Go by yourself. Don't use it to catch up on housework or admin things or taking care of another person. Try to slice out some time for you to wonder what to do with yourself. Let yourself be bored.

Women & Coffee Shops

I am 12
My Mimi brings me.
I slump in a window seat
next to a pile of Romance.
women swoon on the cover,
Fabio-clutched.
Military books for me,
men that look like my father.

I am 16
I bring a date
order cortados, bring poetry
fast ideas
She picks out a couples' devotional
no Song of Songs, all fire & brimstone
complains the coffee isn't sweet enough
I feel the same about the conversation

I am 37
I bring my daughter
She burns her tongue on cocoa
She picks out a woodworking magazine
I order coffee & poetry.

I close the poetry and ask
what her favorite grain of wood is.
I want to have learned something.

Go on a pastry-crawl.

Spend a few days asking everyone you bump into which bakery is their favorite and make a list from there. Are we thinking cookies? Croissants? Pie? Are we searching for the best gluten-free donut? Think of it as a treasure hunt for the recommendations you've collected. Clues to finding the tastiest treats in your town.

> **Tip:** Take a friend or two so you can sample as many pastries as possible. You have our permission to only order one cannoli and share it with three people.

Give It to Me in Analog

news feeds have left you nauseous
gatling guns of information
searing burning punctures
through your soul & focus
burdened your brow with blues

gonna get free
give it to me analog

In the aisle of second hand
book stores,
thumbing pages
loving Lucia Berlin
& Ada Limon
by the lineful.

gonna get free
give it to me analog

Need soundtracks of
tuning strings & whistling
afternoon kettles

gonna get free
give it to me analog

Need a taste-
finger picked-
from a languid day of
hunting & gathering art.
not single-clicked, algorithm manipulated,
cookie directed.
But from that world of bones & wind
of blood & hurt & joy & all that living.

Pay a local poet for a custom work.

Not Josh! That doesn't count. Okay, it counts, but this is about making new connections. It's going to take some research about open mics, and poetry readings. Find a place where you can grab something tasty to drink and listen to some poetry. Or look up some creative writing groups on social media to track down a poet for hire.

Tip: they're almost all for hire.

Splash Pad

Bad news circles like a bloated great white

Elephants have made the summer murderous.

Golden Eagles screeching the same brand of destruction in 1939.

In the fall, did any Polish children take note of the kaleidoscope crunching leaves?

Did a sun headed girl try to keep up with the racing, autumnal wind on a bike?

Did a boy discover poetry in the back of a library - between lessons & pages of ink & hope?

Or was it all tanks and terrible headlines? Was it somehow all of it?

In 2025 - my girls are 10, 6, and 10. They are aware of evil and his many names.

They also know tomatoes off the vine, warmed in July's sun.

They know the purr & croak of a content backyard chicken.

They know dad will ride the tallest water slides should they be too scared and he will shoulder-shimmy-announce: "movie night!"

Our lives are both sharks & splash pads

Bury treasure. Put something in the ground, obscured in public. Be the origin to someone's adventure.

You could sit at a bench in a park and scrape away the rocks and dirt until there's a little hole and in that hole you put something small or shiny and it's right where some day a kid might be sitting on that bench, waiting for their grownups, drawing lines in the dirt with a stick they found and there, peeking out, is a treasure. Something special for them to take home. To slip in their pocket and ponder on the drive back. Something sparking a magical start of a daydream.

Flaunt Flautas

I'm gonna do
the lollygagging
on the graves of
my haters

Get the gravy
ready for this
tatter

Alone, I am
a silly goose.

With your help
we can be a
goofy gaggle.

Full rebellion
in the face of
the daily sledge
hammer of facts
riddling our
collective,
absurd existence.

the void gapes
I wink
the void blushes.

Remind me I
exist in the flesh.
I take my pain
and butter both in
real life, not through
a screen. i am so over

stimulated some days
i can't remember

if
i saw this all in a family
photo album or a meme.

Find a friend to lock arms and skip in public with.

The point of this is to laugh and let go. Go with someone you trust, or someone you barely know. No one looks cool while skipping. Good. Let cool go. Embrace the dork. Embrace the silly. We don't have enough silly moments. Maybe we feel we don't deserve to feel lightness. I disagree. We should have opportunities to feel easy things.

Scenario

A box of greeting cards spilled over in the ocean. For months, the underwater world became sentimental.

Great Whites gave each other graduation cards for slaying large tuna. Tuna gave each other condolence cards for their losses.

Octopi celebrated birthdays, whales observed anniversaries, and seahorses made little notes just because they were thinking of each other.

When the news interviewed a beautiful, multi colored mantis shrimp and asked why the ocean was now prolifically intentional and literate-
the shrimp stated, "we had the feelings, we just didn't have the tools."

The reporter said, "So I guess you could say humans are the real heroes for dumping this trash in your home."

"No," replied the shrimp, "y'all are still really messed up for that."

Write someone a letter and mail it to them.

There was something lost when we ceased passing notes back and forth in class. When we stopped sending each other postcards and writing love letters. And pages long apologies. I'm not saying we should bring back thank you notes, but start smaller. Thinking of you notes. Care about you notes. It occurred to me about you notes. Do you have physical mail saved somewhere in a drawer or a box? Who wrote them to you? What made you keep them? Not sure who to write a letter to? Maybe it's time for a years later reply to one of those notes.

> Tip: Want to get really fancy? Include a self-addressed stamped envelope so they can write you back if they want.

Museum Day

The sign near the entrance explains this used to be someone's home.
A reminder that there will always be people who think they are better than
you.
How else do you explain hallways that could fit a parade of Cadillacs?
A suburb of a bedroom.

The entire property belongs to the public now.
Kind of. Sort of.
If you can pay the entry fee.

An oil barron's home turned
museum feels like revolution.
Kind of. Sort of.

There are truly worse alternatives and I'm being a snot.

Still, the museum gets it
right a lot of the time.
Evenings with music & food.
Hospitality and interesting
People in books on microphones.
I've spent many

stolen afternoons in the lackadaisical gardens,
beauty blooming and splayed out.
Feeling like freedom.
Kind of. Sort of.

Spend a day in a museum and use it to fuel your own creative medium.

Some of us are comfortable in museum settings, others might be more hesitant and that is valid. Be assured that every museum (art, history, science) is full of people who want you there. They want people to step through the doors and experience what they have created. In a history exhibit? Ask yourself what you would have felt at the time. Looking at artwork? Ask yourself what the artist intended you to feel. Find a docent and ask them what their favorite piece/exhibit/area is.

> Tip: Many museums participate in programs that allow members of other museums to visit for a discount or free. Also, check their calendars to see if they have free admission community days!

Evening Routine

Diversion,
moon play,
until morphed

into an antelope,
a river, a deeper
medicine.

oh-
mama, I can
be so many

I'm a
killing floor.

I'm a
rider on the storm.

I'm a
good time for a stipend,

I'm smoke
on the wind

I'm shenanigan
personified

I'm that
impish inclination
to let fly with foolishness
leave your mama
suckin her teeth
"Mhm-ing"
Shenanaigans
lead to open flames,
Dangerous dances
no regard for public safety
when it comes to the playlist.

Co-create something with friends - ekphrastics, murals, potlucks, a band, read each other short stories. Make it normal/regular.

I'm going out on a limb and guessing that when Josh says "make it normal/regular" he meant "do it often and with intention." Though trying to get someone to write a poem or play in a band like a normie could be a really fun prompt as well. ANYWAY there are so many ways to collaborate with your friends. Maybe everyone brings a type of cheese and you put together a charcuterie board. Or you start a giant painting where people you invite add details over the years.

Landline

It was 2003.
Do or Die wanted to know if we could keep it on the low.
J. Lo was telling us love didn't cost a thing,
and Joe wanted to know what turned you on
so he could be the one
to make you smile.

It was 2003.
I had played guitar for exactly four years & four seconds
and believed I could John Mayer my way into any available heart
and my heart set its sights on Jazmine.

But it was 2003
There were no DM's to slyly slide into,
with perfectly curated paragraphs.
There were only landlines
To become entangled
In gatekeeping conversations with relatives.

And for Jazmine's family,
the lion of the landline,
was her father.
And for Jazmine's father, he was a former Marine.
Former being the operative word, but he never got the memo.
If you did not come correct in manners and syntax there was
a high likelihood your rear would end up on a plane,
in less than 12 hours, on its way to Fallujah.
Courtesy of Jazmine's father's boot.

It was high stakes, high anxiety.
I stuttered and stammered & clawed & clamored.
Truth is, if I could find Jazmine's father today,
I would thank him.
There has yet to be a job interview or first date, as intimidating.
Extroverted skills forged in the 90's.

Retro Refrain

Take the refrain or chorus from a song and use it to reflect on your own life. Maybe it's nostalgic and you can weave the details of your memory with your current reflections and conclusions. Maybe it's a current favorite on your playlist and the chorus can be a form of a mantra to get you through life's current season. Music and poetry are close companions, set them loose on the page and let them play together.

Author Bios

Josh Wann (he/him)

Josh Wann is a writer and educator in Tulsa, OK. His plays have been produced by Blackjack Rewrite Company, among others, at Living Arts, The Nightingale Theater, and Studio 308. His essays have been published in *The Black Wall Street Times*, *Calliope Crashes*, and others. Lastly, his poetry and comedy have been performed at various venues and events throughout Tulsa, including The Tulsa Performing Arts Center's Orbit Arts Festival, The Woody Guthrie Center, Living Arts, The Low Down, Arts @302, The Gathering Place, and too many living rooms and parking lots to remember. He gravitates towards laughter, nature, picking the guitar, keeping his chickens, and big plates of breakfast foods.

Jes McCutchen (she/her)

Jes McCutchen (she/her/hers) lives in Tulsa with her partner Marshall, and their son. As well as one stinky weenie dog named Fable Rose. When not writing poetry, she writes queer YA science fiction and fantasy novels that always have happy endings, and makes art. She is currently working on the Geraldine Hart expanded universe. She struggled with postpartum depression and anxiety, and is currently medicated. You can find more information and contact her at *jesmccutchenwrites.com*.

Acknowledgements

Thank you, Jesus. Thank you to my supportive family. Gratitude for Steve and Kelly, for raising me around equal parts nature and books. Thank you for the style, Mimi. Gratitude for my children: Ethan, Olivia, Everly, and Eleanor for your faith and frivolity with all of me. Thank you to my champion, best friend, and partner in the darkest winter through bountiful harvest, Amanda Wann. Thank you to the Collins family. Thank you to the friends who have leaped at all opportunities for a side quest with me. Especially the foxfire gang (Jes, Emily, Amanda), David & Brandon, Jon, Kasey, Frank, Eddie, John, Sam, Adam, Delrina, Cierra, Brad, Joshua, Tyler, Marshall, Kyle, and all the faculty lounges. Thank you to the teachers and mentors that encouraged my writing. Especially Qurayash Ali Lansana, Jeanetta Calhoun Mish, Kat Meads, Kerry Cohen, Brian Cowlishaw, Monique Brinker, and Tim Bradford. Thank you to the venues and community organizers that give poets and artists spaces, opportunities, platforms, and funding. Especially Dr. Joseph Boyne, Amy Rains, Kara Hader, Sterling Matthews, Kode Ransom, Written Quincey, Hank Byrd, Jerica Wortham, Quinn Carver Johnson, Bracken Klar, Lori Lansana, Shawn Crawford, Tony B, Phetote Mshairi, and Nehemiah Frank. And thank you to the kitchens, parks, creeks, woods, cafes, museums, and second-hand book/record stores that supply endless shenanigans and reasons to believe in joy and healing. - **Josh**

Thank you to my family (especially M & G) and my community (especially the poets and beef cakes). Shout out to the foxfire gang and your ceaseless support of my ideas. And to Josh for trusting me with his poetry, even if I had to basically beg. To Tulsa and all the spaces people make for creativity, particularly M.U.S.T. and Heirloom Rustic Ales. To Tina, Sam, and Sarah who always encourage me to create. All we have is our creativity and each other and I'm ready to wield that like a sword if it means filling us with love and art and community. Look out for one another and yourselves. – **Jes**